CABO SAN LUCAS

A Traveler's Guide to Paradise

By

C.J John

TABLE OF CONTENT

Introduction to Cabo San Lucas

Located at the southern tip of Mexico's Baja California Peninsula, Cabo San Lucas stands as a testament to the stunning natural beauty and vibrant culture of the region. With its sun-kissed beaches, crystalline waters, and dramatic landscapes, this picturesque destination has captivated travelers for generations. From the azure waves of the Sea of Cortez to the rugged terrain of the desert, Cabo San Lucas offers a diverse array of experiences waiting to be discovered.

Aerial view

Street view

Geography and Climate

Cabo San Lucas is situated in the state of Baja California Sur, occupying the southernmost tip of the Baja California Peninsula. Bordered by the Pacific Ocean to the west and the Sea of Cortez to the east, the region boasts a unique geography characterized by rugged coastlines, towering cliffs, and expansive desert plains. The climate in Cabo San Lucas is arid, with year-round sunshine and minimal rainfall. Temperatures vary depending on the season, with hot summers and mild winters attracting visitors throughout the year.

History and Heritage

The history of Cabo San Lucas is as rich and diverse as its landscape. Originally inhabited by indigenous tribes such as the Pericúes and the Guaycuras, the region later became a point of interest for Spanish explorers in the 16th century. The arrival of Spanish conquistadors brought about significant changes, including the establishment of missions and settlements along the coast. Over the centuries, Cabo San Lucas has evolved into a vibrant cultural melting pot, blending indigenous traditions with Spanish influences and modern innovations.

Tourism and Attractions

In recent decades, Cabo San Lucas has emerged as a premier tourist destination, attracting visitors from around the globe with its unparalleled beauty and abundance of attractions. One of the most iconic landmarks in Cabo San Lucas is El Arco, a natural stone arch formation that marks the meeting point of the Pacific Ocean and the Sea of Cortez. This stunning geological wonder is a must-see for visitors, offering breathtaking views and photo opportunities.

Beyond El Arco, Cabo San Lucas boasts an array of attractions and activities to suit every interest and preference. Beach lovers can soak up the sun on the pristine shores of Médano Beach, while adventure seekers can explore the underwater wonders of the Sea of Cortez through snorkeling or scuba diving. Sport fishing enthusiasts flock to Cabo San Lucas to test their skills against the abundant marine life, with opportunities to catch prized species such as marlin, dorado, and tuna

Medano beach

Culture and Traditions

Cabo San Lucas is steeped in a rich tapestry of culture and traditions, reflecting its diverse heritage and influences. The local population is known for its warmth and hospitality, welcoming visitors with open arms and sharing their customs and traditions. Festivals and celebrations are an integral part of life in Cabo San Lucas, with events such as the Feast of Saint Luke and the Festival Gastrovino showcasing the region's culinary delights and artistic talents.

The cuisine of Cabo San Lucas is a reflection of its coastal location and abundant seafood. Fresh fish, shrimp, and lobster are staples of the local diet, often prepared with traditional spices and flavors. Visitors can sample a variety of dishes, from fish tacos and ceviche to seafood cocktails and grilled octopus, paired with refreshing margaritas or ice-cold cervezas.

Accommodations and Hospitality

Cabo San Lucas offers a wide range of accommodations to suit every budget and preference, from luxury resorts and boutique hotels to cozy bed and breakfasts and vacation rentals. Many resorts in Cabo San Lucas boast world-class amenities, including infinity pools, spa facilities, and gourmet dining options, ensuring a comfortable and memorable stay for guests.

In addition to traditional accommodations, Cabo San Lucas also offers unique lodging experiences, such as beachfront villas, eco-friendly resorts, and glamping sites nestled in the desert. Whether you're seeking a romantic retreat, a family-friendly getaway, or an adventure-filled vacation, Cabo San Lucas has something for everyone.

Practical Travel Information

For travelers planning a trip to Cabo San Lucas, it's essential to be prepared with practical travel information and tips. The main airport serving the region is Los Cabos International Airport (SJD), located approximately 30 minutes from downtown Cabo San Lucas. Visitors can also arrive by cruise ship or bus, with options for ground transportation available upon arrival.

Currency in Cabo San Lucas is the Mexican peso (MXN), although U.S. dollars are widely accepted at hotels, restaurants, and shops. It's advisable to exchange currency at banks or currency exchange offices to ensure the best rates. Spanish is the official language spoken in Cabo San Lucas, although English is widely spoken in tourist areas.

Safety is a top priority for travelers visiting Cabo San Lucas. While the region is generally considered safe for tourists, it's essential to take common-sense precautions, such as staying aware of your surroundings, avoiding isolated areas at night, and safeguarding personal belongings. Medical facilities and emergency services are available in Cabo San Lucas, with hospitals and clinics equipped to handle a range of medical issues.

Cabo San Lucas embodies the essence of paradise, with its breathtaking scenery, vibrant culture, and warm hospitality. Whether you're seeking relaxation on the beach, adrenaline-fueled adventures, or cultural immersion, Cabo San Lucas offers an unforgettable vacation experience. From the iconic landmarks of El Arco to the bustling streets of downtown, this enchanting destination invites travelers to discover the magic of the Baja California Peninsula, Cabo San Lucas.

SOME MAJOR NEIGHBORHOODS

Exploring the Enchanting Marina in Cabo San Lucas

MARINA view 1

*MARINA*view2

Nestled along the breathtaking coastline of Baja California Sur, the marina in Cabo San Lucas stands as a vibrant hub of activity, offering a fusion of natural beauty, maritime adventures, and lively entertainment. Here's a glimpse into the allure of this captivating destination:

- **A Gateway to Adventure**
  The marina serves as a gateway to a myriad of adventures awaiting in the azure waters of the Pacific Ocean and the Sea of Cortez. From here, travelers embark on fishing excursions, snorkeling escapades, and thrilling boat tours to iconic landmarks like the famous Arch of Cabo San Lucas and the pristine Lover's Beach.

- **Spectacular Views**
  As the sun dips below the horizon, casting a golden glow over the marina's waters, visitors are treated to a spectacle of nature's beauty. The vibrant hues of the sunset paint the sky in a mesmerizing palette of oranges, pinks, and purples, creating a postcard-perfect backdrop for an evening stroll along the promenade.

- **Epicurean Delights**
  Nestled along the marina's edge are an array of waterfront restaurants and cafes, where travelers can indulge in the fresh flavors of Baja cuisine while savoring panoramic views of the ocean. From freshly caught seafood to authentic Mexican dishes, the culinary offerings here are as diverse as they are delicious.

- **Shopping and Entertainment**
  The marina is also a bustling hub of shopping and entertainment, with an eclectic mix of boutiques, souvenir shops, and art galleries lining its cobblestone streets. Visitors can peruse handcrafted treasures, shop for designer labels, or simply soak in the vibrant atmosphere as live music fills the air.

- **Charter Opportunities**
  For those seeking the ultimate luxury experience, the marina offers a selection of private yacht charters, allowing guests to explore the coastline in style and comfort. Whether it's a romantic sunset cruise or a day of island hopping, these charter services cater to every whim and desire.

- **A Vibrant Atmosphere**
  Day or night, the marina exudes a palpable energy that
  draws travelers from near and far. Whether it's the bustling
  activity of fishing boats returning with their day's catch or the
  infectious rhythms of live music drifting from waterfront bars,
  there's never a dull moment in this lively waterfront district.

  The marina in Cabo San Lucas is a captivating destination that
seamlessly blends natural beauty, maritime adventure, and
vibrant culture. Whether you're seeking outdoor excitement,
epicurean delights, or simply a place to unwind and soak in the
scenery, this enchanting waterfront district offers something for
everyone.

PEDREGAL

Discovering the Charms of Pedregal
Cabo San Lucas's Premier Luxury Community

Waldorf Astoria Los cabos pedregal

Pedregal real Estate

Resort pedregal

Los Cabos rentals

Discovering the Charms of Pedregal:
Cabo San Lucas's Premier Luxury Community

Nestled on the southern tip of the Baja California Peninsula, overlooking the azure waters of the Pacific Ocean, Pedregal stands as one of Cabo San Lucas's most prestigious and exclusive residential communities. Steeped in luxury and surrounded by natural beauty, Pedregal offers residents and visitors alike a haven of tranquility and sophistication. Here's a closer look at the allure of Pedregal:

Unparalleled Views

Perched atop rugged cliffs overlooking the Pacific, Pedregal boasts unrivaled panoramic views that stretch as far as the eye can see. From its elevated vantage point, residents are treated to breathtaking vistas of the ocean, the iconic Arch of Cabo San Lucas, and the rugged desert landscape that surrounds the community.

Luxurious Residences

Pedregal is renowned for its opulent residences, which range from sprawling hilltop villas to luxurious beachfront estates as seen in the above views. Designed with the utmost attention to detail and featuring state-of-the-art amenities, these homes epitomize the epitome of luxury living in Cabo San Lucas.

Exclusive Amenities

Residents of Pedregal enjoy access to a wealth of exclusive amenities designed to enhance their lifestyle and elevate their experience. From private beach clubs and gourmet restaurants to tennis courts and spa facilities, every aspect of life in Pedregal is imbued with luxury and refinement.

Natural Beauty

Despite its reputation for luxury, Pedregal remains deeply connected to its natural surroundings. The community is dotted with lush gardens, winding pathways, and scenic overlooks, allowing residents to immerse themselves in the beauty of the Baja landscape.

Privacy and Security

Privacy and security are paramount in Pedregal, with 24-hour gated access and a dedicated security team ensuring the safety and tranquility of residents. This sense of seclusion allows residents to relax and unwind in an atmosphere of complete serenity.

Proximity to Amenities

Despite its secluded location, Pedregal is just minutes away from the vibrant heart of Cabo San Lucas, where residents can enjoy world-class dining, shopping, and entertainment options. Whether it's a gourmet meal at a Michelin-starred restaurant or a night out on the town, everything you could possibly desire is within easy reach.

Pedregal stands as a testament to luxury living in Cabo San Lucas, offering residents an unparalleled blend of natural beauty, exclusive amenities, and unparalleled privacy and security. Whether you're seeking a permanent residence or a vacation retreat, Pedregal promises a lifestyle of unparalleled sophistication and refinement.

San Jose del Cabo

At the southern tip of Mexico's Baja California Peninsula lies a hidden gem awaiting discovery: San Jose del Cabo. Tucked away from the bustling tourist crowds of Cabo San Lucas, this charming town exudes a tranquil ambiance, rich history, and breathtaking natural beauty. Join us on a journey to explore the many wonders of San Jose del Cabo, where colonial architecture, cultural heritage, culinary delights, outdoor adventures, and pristine beaches await.

view 1

view2

view3

view4

A Glimpse into History: Exploring San Jose del Cabo's Colonial Charm

Stepping into the heart of San Jose del Cabo feels like stepping back in time. The town's historic downtown area is a labyrinth of cobblestone streets flanked by elegant colonial buildings, each bearing witness to centuries of history. At the center of it all stands the iconic Mission San Jose del Cabo Anuiti, a stunning example of Spanish colonial architecture dating back to the 18th century. Visitors can wander through the mission's tranquil courtyard, adorned with lush gardens and a serene fountain, while admiring the intricate details of its Baroque façade.

Cultural Immersion: Embracing Art, Music, and Tradition

San Jose del Cabo is not only a feast for the eyes but also a cultural haven waiting to be explored. The town's vibrant art district is a testament to its creative spirit, with numerous galleries and studios showcasing the works of local and international artists. From contemporary paintings and sculptures to traditional Mexican crafts, there's something to captivate every art lover's imagination. Visitors can also immerse themselves in the rhythms of Mexican music and dance at lively festivals and performances held throughout the year, celebrating the region's rich cultural heritage.

Culinary Delights: A Gastronomic Journey Through Baja Cuisine

No visit to San Jose del Cabo is complete without indulging in its culinary delights. The town's burgeoning food scene offers a tantalizing array of flavors, blending traditional Mexican cuisine with international influences. Seafood lovers can savor the freshest catches of the day at waterfront restaurants overlooking the azure waters of the Sea of Cortez, while street food aficionados can sample an array of mouthwatering tacos, tamales, and ceviches at local markets and food stalls. For those seeking a more upscale dining experience, San Jose del Cabo boasts an array of gourmet restaurants helmed by talented chefs, serving up innovative dishes crafted from locally sourced ingredients.

Beach Bliss: Sun, Sand, and Serenity

With its miles of pristine coastline and turquoise waters, San Jose del Cabo is a beach lover's paradise. From secluded coves to bustling strips of sand, there's a beach to suit every mood and preference. Playa Palmilla beckons with its calm waters and swaying palm trees, perfect for swimming, snorkeling, or simply basking in the sun. Surfers flock to the breaks of Costa Azul and Zippers, where the waves are consistently epic and the vibe is laid-back and unpretentious. And for those seeking ultimate relaxation, a day spent lounging on the golden sands of Playa del Amor is pure bliss, with nothing but the sound of the waves lulling you into a state of pure tranquility.

Outdoor Adventures: Exploring the Natural Wonders of Baja

Beyond its beautiful beaches and historic charm, San Jose del Cabo offers a wealth of outdoor adventures just waiting to be discovered. Adventurous souls can explore the rugged beauty of the Baja desert on thrilling ATV or off-road tours, traversing dusty trails and rocky terrain while taking in panoramic views of the surrounding landscape. For adrenaline junkies, zip-lining through the canopy of a pristine desert oasis provides an exhilarating rush unlike any other, while eco-tours offer a chance to encounter the region's diverse wildlife, from desert reptiles to majestic whales. And for those seeking a more leisurely pace, a sunset cruise along the coastline offers the perfect opportunity to relax and unwind while taking in the breathtaking beauty of the Sea of Cortez.

Retail Therapy: Shopping for Treasures in San Jose del Cabo

No trip to San Jose del Cabo would be complete without a bit of retail therapy. The town's quaint streets are lined with an eclectic mix of shops and boutiques, offering everything from handcrafted jewelry and textiles to unique souvenirs and keepsakes. Artisanal markets and galleries are a treasure trove of local craftsmanship, showcasing the work of talented artisans and designers from across the region. Whether you're searching for the perfect souvenir to commemorate your trip or simply looking to indulge in a bit of shopping therapy, San Jose del Cabo has something for everyone.

Planning Your Visit: Practical Tips and Recommendations

Before embarking on your journey to San Jose del Cabo, it's important to plan ahead and make the most of your time in this enchanting destination. Here are a few practical tips and recommendations to help you plan your trip:

Best Time to Visit: San Jose del Cabo enjoys a warm and sunny climate year-round, making it an ideal destination for travelers seeking sunshine and relaxation. The peak tourist season typically runs from December to April when temperatures are pleasantly warm, and rainfall is minimal. However, visitors can also enjoy discounted rates and fewer crowds during the shoulder seasons of spring and fall.

Getting There: San Jose del Cabo is easily accessible via Los Cabos International Airport (SJD), located just a short drive from the town center. Many major airlines offer direct flights to Los Cabos from cities across the United States, Canada, and Mexico, making it convenient to reach this tropical paradise.

Accommodations: From luxury resorts to boutique hotels and charming bed and breakfasts, San Jose del Cabo offers a wide range of accommodations to suit every budget and preference. Whether you're seeking a beachfront retreat, a romantic hideaway, or a family-friendly resort, you'll find plenty of options to choose from.

Transportation: While San Jose del Cabo is easily navigable on foot, renting a car or booking guided tours can provide added convenience and flexibility for exploring the surrounding area. Taxis and rideshare services are also readily available for short trips within town.

Safety and Security: Like any travel destination, it's important to exercise caution and be aware of your surroundings while visiting San Jose del Cabo. While the town is generally safe for tourists, it's advisable to take common-sense precautions such as avoiding isolated areas at night and keeping valuables secure.

Local Customs and Etiquette: San Jose del Cabo is known for its warm and welcoming hospitality, and visitors are encouraged to embrace the local customs and etiquette during their stay. Tipping is customary in restaurants and for other services, and a small gratuity is always appreciated for exceptional service.

From its colonial charm and cultural heritage to its culinary delights, outdoor adventures, and pristine beaches, San Jose del Cabo offers a wealth of experiences just waiting to be discovered. Whether you're seeking relaxation, adventure, romance, or cultural immersion, this enchanting destination has something for everyone. So pack your bags, leave your worries behind, and embark on a journey to San Jose del Cabo, where unforgettable memories await.

TOURIST CORRIDOR

Nestled between the azure waters of the Sea of Cortez and the rugged beauty of the Baja California desert, the tourist corridor of Cabo San Lucas beckons with its unparalleled charm. Stretching along the southern tip of the Baja Peninsula, this enchanting corridor seamlessly blends natural wonders, luxurious resorts, and authentic Mexican culture. Let's embark on a captivating journey through the sun-kissed landscapes and vibrant experiences that define this idyllic destination.

Coastal Splendor
The tourist corridor of Cabo San Lucas boasts some of the most stunning coastal vistas in the world. With miles of pristine beaches, secluded coves, and dramatic cliffs, it's a paradise for sun-seekers and adventurers alike. Lounge on the golden sands

of Medano Beach, embark on a snorkeling excursion to explore vibrant coral reefs, or set sail on a sunset cruise along the shimmering waters, where the horizon meets the sky in a mesmerizing display of colors.

Luxurious Resorts:

Indulge in the epitome of relaxation and luxury at the world-class resorts that dot the coastline of Cabo San Lucas. From lavish beachfront villas to boutique hotels nestled in secluded oases, each accommodation offers a sanctuary of serenity and sophistication. Pamper yourself with rejuvenating spa treatments, savor gourmet cuisine crafted from fresh local ingredients, and unwind in opulent suites with panoramic views of the ocean, ensuring an unforgettable retreat.

Outdoor Adventures

For thrill-seekers and nature enthusiasts, the tourist corridor of Cabo San Lucas is a playground of outdoor adventures. Embark on a thrilling ATV excursion through desert trails, zip-line across breathtaking canyons, or go whale watching to witness the majestic beauty of humpback whales breaching in the open waters. With activities ranging from snorkeling and scuba diving to horseback riding and hiking, there's no shortage of adrenaline-pumping experiences to be had.

Cultural Experiences

Delve into the rich tapestry of Mexican culture as you explore the quaint towns and vibrant markets along the tourist corridor. Wander through the cobblestone streets of San Jose del Cabo, where colonial architecture blends seamlessly with colorful art galleries and charming cafes. Sample traditional Mexican cuisine at local eateries, browse artisanal crafts at the Mercado Mexicano, and immerse yourself in the lively rhythms of mariachi music and folkloric dances, celebrating the spirit of Mexico.

Marine Marvels

Explore the underwater wonders that thrive beneath the surface of the Sea of Cortez, often referred to as the "Aquarium of the World" by Jacques Cousteau. Snorkel alongside tropical fish and sea turtles in Cabo Pulmo National Park, home to one of the oldest coral reefs in the Americas. Dive into the depths of Cabo San Lucas Marine Park, where vibrant coral formations and diverse marine life await, including playful sea lions and graceful manta rays, offering an unforgettable glimpse into the underwater realm.

The tourist corridor of Cabo San Lucas is a symphony of natural beauty, luxury, adventure, and culture, inviting travelers to embark on a transformative journey that captivates the senses and nourishes the soul. Whether indulging in the blissful tranquility of beachside retreats, embarking on adrenaline-fueled escapades, or immersing oneself in the vibrant tapestry of Mexican culture, every moment spent in this idyllic destination is an opportunity to create cherished memories that last a lifetime. So, come discover the magic of Cabo San Lucas and let its timeless allure captivate your heart.

TODOS SANTOS

Todos Santos is actually a town located in Baja California Sur, Mexico, rather than in Cabo San Lucas specifically. However, it is within the general region of the tourist corridor that encompasses Cabo San Lucas, San Jose del Cabo, and the area in between.

Todos Santos: A Gem in the Baja Peninsula

Todos Santos, often referred to as "Pueblo Mágico" (Magical Town), is a charming oasis nestled between the Pacific Ocean and the Sierra de la Laguna mountains. Despite being approximately 50 miles north of Cabo San Lucas, it's a popular day trip destination for visitors exploring the southern tip of the Baja Peninsula.

views

Elfado beach

Highlights of Todos Santos

Art and Culture: Todos Santos has a thriving arts scene, with numerous galleries, studios, and workshops showcasing the work of local and international artists. Visitors can explore colorful murals adorning the town's streets, browse handcrafted pottery and textiles, and immerse themselves in the creative energy that permeates the community.

Historical Landmarks: The town is steeped in history, with well-preserved colonial architecture and historic buildings dating back to the 18th century. Notable landmarks include the iconic Mission Santa Rosa de Todos Santos, a beautiful example of Spanish colonial architecture, and the historic district filled with quaint shops and cafes.

Culinary Delights: Todos Santos is renowned for its culinary scene, offering a diverse array of dining options ranging from upscale restaurants to casual eateries. Visitors can sample fresh seafood dishes, traditional Mexican cuisine, and international fare, all made with locally sourced ingredients.

Surfing and Beaches: The nearby coastline boasts pristine beaches and world-class surf breaks, making it a haven for surfers and beachgoers alike. Playa Los Cerritos is a popular spot for swimming, surfing, and sunbathing, with its golden sands and turquoise waters providing the perfect backdrop for relaxation.

Ecotourism and Outdoor Activities: Surrounding the town are rugged desert landscapes, lush oases, and pristine nature reserves waiting to be explored. Outdoor enthusiasts can embark on hiking and mountain biking adventures, birdwatching excursions, and guided tours to discover the region's diverse flora and fauna.

While Todos Santos is distinct from Cabo San Lucas, it offers a unique and authentic experience that complements the vibrant energy of the tourist corridor. Whether exploring its cultural landmarks, indulging in culinary delights, or immersing oneself in its natural beauty, a visit to Todos Santos promises unforgettable memories and a deeper appreciation for the enchanting diversity of the Baja Peninsula.

SOME BEST PLACES WITH SCENIC VIEWS IN CABO SAN LUCAS

WALDORF ASTORIA RESORT LOS CABOS PEDREGAL

view1

view2

view3

view4

view5

EL FARALLON CABO

view1

view2

DON MANUEL'S PEDREGAL

Don emmanuel's restaurant, waldorf, Pedregal: view1

Don emmanuel's restaurant, waldorf, Pedregal: view2

SANDOS FINISTERRA RESORT

view1

view2

view3

CASA DORADA LOS CABO RESORT AND SPA

view1

view2

view3

GRAND SOLMAR LAND'S END RESORT & SPA

view1

view2

view3

view4

view5

view6

view7

FINISTERRA RESORT CABO

view1

view2

view3

view4

view5

HOTEL TESORO LOS CABO

view1

view2

view4

view5

view6

view7

view8

view9

PUEBLO BONITO SUNSET BEACH

view1

view2

view3

view4

view5

view6

view7

view7

JOURNEY TO CABO SAN LUCAS

FLIGHT JOURNEY

Whether you're arriving from a nearby city or traveling from across the globe, flying into Cabo San Lucas offers convenience and efficiency, setting the stage for an unforgettable vacation experience.

Airport Accessibility
Los Cabos International Airport (SJD): Serving both Cabo San Lucas and its sister city, San José del Cabo, SJD is the main gateway to the region. Located just a short drive from downtown Cabo San Lucas, the airport offers easy access to the area's top attractions and accommodations.

Direct Flights
Domestic Flights: Major airlines offer direct flights to Los Cabos International Airport from cities across Mexico, including Mexico City, Guadalajara, and Monterrey. With frequent and convenient connections, travelers can reach Cabo San Lucas from virtually anywhere in the country with ease.
International Flights: Los Cabos International Airport also welcomes flights from numerous international destinations, including the United States, Canada, and Europe. Popular routes connect Cabo San Lucas to cities such as Los Angeles, Dallas, Calgary, and London, making it accessible to travelers from around the world.

Airlines and Services

Full-Service Carriers: Major airlines such as American Airlines, Delta Air Lines, United Airlines, and Aeromexico offer regular service to Los Cabos International Airport, providing passengers with a range of options for comfort, convenience, and amenities.
Low-Cost Carriers: Budget-conscious travelers can take advantage of offerings from low-cost carriers like Southwest Airlines, Frontier Airlines, and Volaris, which provide affordable options for flying to Cabo San Lucas without compromising on quality or service.

Airport Facilities

- *Modern Amenities*: Los Cabos International Airport boasts modern facilities and amenities to enhance the travel experience for passengers. From duty-free shopping and dining options to VIP lounges and car rental services, the airport provides everything you need for a seamless arrival and departure.
- *Transportation Options*: Upon landing at Los Cabos International Airport, travelers can easily access transportation options to reach their final destination in Cabo San Lucas. Taxis, shuttle services, and rental cars are readily available, ensuring convenient onward travel to hotels, resorts, and attractions.

Flying to Cabo San Lucas is a breeze, thanks to the accessibility and convenience of Los Cabos International Airport. With direct flights from domestic and international destinations, travelers can easily reach this tropical paradise and begin their adventure in no time. So sit back, relax, and get ready to experience the beauty and excitement of Cabo San Lucas from the moment you touch down at the airport.

SEA JOURNEY

Getting to Cabo San Lucas by Sea

For those seeking a truly unforgettable journey, arriving in Cabo San Lucas by sea is an experience like no other. Whether you're a seasoned sailor or embarking on a luxury cruise, the stunning coastline and azure waters of the Baja Peninsula set the stage for a memorable approach to this vibrant destination. From private yachts to cruise ships, there are various ways to sail into Cabo San Lucas, each offering its own unique charm and allure.

Private Yacht or Sailboat
- **Charter Services:** Embark on a private yacht or sailboat charter from nearby marinas such as Marina Cabo San Lucas or Marina Puerto Los Cabos. With experienced captains and crew at your service, you can enjoy a personalized and luxurious journey along the coast, complete with breathtaking views and exclusive access to secluded coves and beaches.
- **Coastal Cruising:** Set sail from nearby ports such as San Diego or Ensenada and cruise down the scenic coastline of the Baja Peninsula en route to Cabo San Lucas. Take in the rugged beauty of the desert landscape, with opportunities for wildlife spotting and exploration along the way.

Cruise Ships
- **Luxury Cruises:** Indulge in the ultimate getaway aboard a luxury cruise ship bound for Cabo San Lucas. From gourmet dining and world-class entertainment to lavish

accommodations and onboard amenities, luxury cruise lines offer an unparalleled experience of comfort and sophistication.

- **Mainstream Cruises:** Join a mainstream cruise line and set sail on an exciting journey to Cabo San Lucas as part of a larger itinerary. With stops at other popular ports of call along the Mexican Riviera or the Pacific coast, these cruises offer a diverse range of activities and excursions for passengers of all ages and interests.

Sailing Adventures

- **Sailboat Tours:** Join a guided sailing tour departing from Cabo San Lucas and explore the region's pristine waters and coastal scenery. Whether you're interested in a leisurely sunset cruise or an exhilarating sailing excursion, experienced captains and knowledgeable guides will ensure a safe and memorable voyage.
- **Catamaran Expeditions:** Hop aboard a spacious catamaran and set out on an unforgettable adventure along the coast of Cabo San Lucas. With ample deck space for lounging and sunbathing, as well as opportunities for snorkeling, swimming, and wildlife encounters, catamaran tours offer a fun and exhilarating way to experience the beauty of the Baja Peninsula.

Arriving in Cabo San Lucas by sea is a magical experience that sets the tone for an unforgettable vacation in paradise. Whether you choose to sail aboard a private yacht, embark on a luxury cruise, or join a guided sailing tour, the journey itself becomes an integral part of the adventure. So cast off your lines, feel the sea breeze on your face, and get ready to discover the beauty and excitement of Cabo San Lucas from the water.

LAND JOURNEY

Embarking on a road trip to Cabo San Lucas offers travelers the opportunity to immerse themselves in the breathtaking landscapes, charming towns, and rich cultural heritage of the Baja Peninsula. Whether you're driving from nearby cities or embarking on an epic cross-country adventure, the journey to Cabo by land promises unforgettable experiences and the freedom to explore at your own pace.

Scenic Driving Routes
- **Baja California Highway 1 (Carretera Transpeninsular):** Known as the "Mexican Route 66," Highway 1 runs the length of the Baja Peninsula, offering stunning views of the desert, mountains, and coastline along the way. From bustling cities to sleepy fishing villages, this iconic highway showcases the diverse beauty and cultural richness of the region.
- **Pacific Coast Highway (Highway 19):** For travelers approaching Cabo San Lucas from the north, Highway 19 provides a scenic coastal route that hugs the Pacific Ocean. Pass through picturesque seaside towns, pristine beaches, and rugged cliffs, with opportunities for whale watching and beachside dining along the route.

Border Crossings and Entry Requirements
- **Mexico Entry Requirements:** Before embarking on your journey to Cabo San Lucas, familiarize yourself with Mexico's entry requirements, including passport validity, visa regulations, and vehicle permits if driving your own car into

the country. Additionally, be prepared to go through customs and immigration checkpoints at border crossings.

- **Border Crossing Tips:** Plan your border crossing strategically to avoid peak traffic times, and consider obtaining Mexican auto insurance to ensure coverage while driving in Mexico. Be sure to have all necessary documents, including vehicle registration and driver's license, readily accessible for inspection.

Pit Stops and Attractions

- **Ensenada:** As you make your way southward along the Baja Peninsula, consider stopping in Ensenada, a charming coastal town known for its delicious seafood, local wineries, and vibrant cultural scene. Explore the bustling fish market, sample fresh ceviche, or take a scenic drive along the Baja Wine Route.
- **Todos Santos:** Nestled between the Pacific Ocean and the Sierra de la Laguna mountains, Todos Santos is a picturesque oasis renowned for its art galleries, colonial architecture, and laid-back vibe. Stroll through the historic town center, visit the iconic Hotel California, or relax on the pristine beaches nearby.

Safety and Logistics

- **Travel Precautions:** While road tripping in Mexico can be a rewarding experience, it's essential to exercise caution and stay informed about safety conditions along your route. Stay updated on travel advisories, avoid driving at night in remote areas, and exercise common sense when interacting with locals and navigating unfamiliar terrain.

- **Accommodations and Services:** Plan your journey with consideration for accommodations, fuel stations, and services along the way. From budget-friendly motels to luxury resorts, Cabo San Lucas offers a range of lodging options to suit every traveler's preferences and budget.

Embarking on a road trip to Cabo San Lucas by land opens up a world of adventure, allowing travelers to discover the beauty and charm of the Baja Peninsula at their own pace. From scenic driving routes and cultural attractions to safety tips and logistical considerations, a journey to Cabo by land promises unforgettable experiences and the freedom to explore off the beaten path. So pack your bags, hit the road, and get ready to embark on an epic adventure to the southern tip of the Baja Peninsula.

A Guide to Accommodation Options in Cabo San Lucas

Cabo San Lucas, with its stunning beaches, vibrant nightlife, and adventurous spirit, offers a wide range of accommodation options to suit every traveler's preferences and budget. From luxurious resorts and boutique hotels to budget-friendly rentals and charming guesthouses, finding the perfect place to stay in Cabo is easy. Here's a guide to help you navigate the diverse array of accommodation options in this tropical paradise.

Luxury Resorts

Experience ultimate relaxation and indulgence at one of Cabo San Lucas's luxurious resorts. From beachfront properties with infinity pools to cliffside retreats with panoramic views, these resorts offer world-class amenities, impeccable service, and unparalleled comfort. Enjoy gourmet dining, pampering spa treatments, and exclusive access to private beaches and upscale facilities.

Boutique Hotels

Discover the charm and character of Cabo San Lucas's boutique hotels, where personalized service and unique design elements create a memorable stay. Located in the heart of the city or nestled in secluded enclaves, these intimate properties offer stylish accommodations, authentic local experiences, and a warm, welcoming atmosphere. Explore boutique hotels with rooftop terraces, courtyard gardens, or beachfront settings, each offering its own distinct ambiance and flair.

All-Inclusive Resorts

For travelers seeking convenience and value, all-inclusive resorts in Cabo San Lucas provide the perfect solution. With everything from accommodations and meals to activities and entertainment included in one upfront price, these resorts offer a hassle-free vacation experience. Enjoy unlimited dining options, complimentary drinks, and a wide range of recreational activities, from water sports and fitness classes to live music and evening shows.

Vacation Rentals

Enjoy the comforts of home away from home with a vacation rental in Cabo San Lucas. Whether you're looking for a cozy condo, a spacious villa, or a beachfront bungalow, vacation rentals offer flexibility, privacy, and the freedom to create your own itinerary. Ideal for families, groups, or couples seeking a more independent travel experience, vacation rentals provide fully equipped kitchens, living areas, and outdoor spaces for relaxation and enjoyment.

Budget-Friendly Accommodations

Travelers on a budget will find plenty of affordable lodging options in Cabo San Lucas, including budget hotels, hostels, and guesthouses. While these accommodations may offer simpler amenities and fewer frills compared to luxury resorts, they provide comfortable and convenient lodging at a fraction of the cost. Look for budget-friendly accommodations in downtown Cabo San Lucas or in the surrounding areas, where you can enjoy proximity to attractions, dining, and nightlife without breaking the bank.

Whether you're seeking luxury, charm, convenience, or value, Cabo San Lucas offers a diverse array of accommodation options to suit every taste and budget. From lavish resorts and boutique hotels to vacation rentals and budget-friendly lodgings, finding the perfect place to stay is easy in this tropical paradise. So choose your ideal accommodation, pack your bags, and get ready to experience the beauty and excitement of Cabo San Lucas in style.

ACTIVITIES TO ENJOY IN CABO SAN LUCAS

From thrilling outdoor activities and water sports to cultural exploration and relaxation, Cabo offers a diverse range of experiences to suit every taste and interest. Here's a guide to some of the most unforgettable things to do in Cabo San Lucas.

Land Adventures

- ATV Tours: Embark on an off-road adventure through the desert landscape surrounding Cabo San Lucas. Ride through sandy dunes, rugged trails, and dry riverbeds, taking in panoramic views of the Baja Peninsula along the way.
- Zip-lining: Soar through the air on exhilarating zip-line tours that offer bird's-eye views of Cabo's stunning scenery. Feel the rush of adrenaline as you glide over canyons, forests, and rock formations, enjoying an unforgettable perspective of the landscape.
- Hiking: Lace up your hiking boots and explore the natural beauty of Cabo San Lucas on foot. Trek along scenic trails such as the Lovers Beach Trail or the Mount Solmar Trail, where you can enjoy breathtaking views of the coastline and encounter local flora and fauna.

Water Adventures

- Snorkeling and Scuba Diving: Dive into the crystal-clear waters of the Sea of Cortez and discover a vibrant underwater world teeming with marine life. Explore colorful coral reefs, swim alongside tropical fish, and encounter majestic creatures like sea turtles, manta rays, and whale sharks.

- Sport Fishing: Cast your line into the rich waters of the Pacific Ocean and the Sea of Cortez, known for their abundance of game fish. Whether you're a novice angler or a seasoned pro, Cabo offers world-class sport fishing opportunities, with the chance to reel in marlin, tuna, dorado, and more.
- Whale Watching: Embark on a whale watching excursion during the winter months (December to April) and witness the incredible migration of humpback whales. Observe these magnificent creatures breaching, spouting, and playing in the waters off the coast of Cabo San Lucas, creating memories that will last a lifetime.

Cultural Exploration

- Visit the Marina: Stroll along the bustling Marina Cabo San Lucas and soak in the vibrant atmosphere of this waterfront promenade. Admire luxury yachts, browse shops and boutiques, and dine at waterfront restaurants offering fresh seafood and stunning views.
- Explore San José del Cabo: Take a day trip to the nearby town of San José del Cabo and immerse yourself in its colonial charm and cultural heritage. Wander through the historic town center, visit art galleries and museums, and sample authentic Mexican cuisine at local eateries.
- Sunset Cruise: Set sail on a romantic sunset cruise and watch as the sky transforms into a canvas of brilliant colors. Sip cocktails, listen to live music, and enjoy breathtaking

*views of the Pacific Ocean as the sun dips below the horizon,
creating a magical end to your day in Cabo San Lucas.*

From thrilling adventures and water sports to cultural exploration and relaxation, Cabo San Lucas offers a wealth of unforgettable experiences for travelers of all ages and interests. Whether you're seeking adrenaline-pumping activities or serene moments of tranquility, Cabo has something for everyone to enjoy.

Excitement at the beach

Excitement at the beach

Savory Delights: Dining and Cuisine in Cabo San Lucas

Cabo San Lucas isn't just a destination for sun-soaked beaches and thrilling adventures—it's also a culinary haven that tantalizes the taste buds with a diverse array of flavors and cuisines. From fresh seafood and traditional Mexican dishes to international fare and gourmet delights, Cabo's dining scene offers something to satisfy every palate. Join us as we explore the vibrant world of dining and cuisine in Cabo San Lucas.

Local Cuisine

- **Mexican Delights:** Indulge in the vibrant flavors of Mexican cuisine, with dishes ranging from savory tacos and hearty tamales to zesty ceviche and flavorful mole. Don't miss out on regional specialties like fish tacos, shrimp aguachile, and carne asada, prepared with locally sourced ingredients and traditional cooking techniques.

Savory tacos

Hearty tamales

ceviche

- **Baja Cuisine:** Sample the distinctive flavors of Baja
  California cuisine, characterized by its emphasis on fresh
  seafood, citrus fruits, and Mediterranean influences. Savor
  dishes such as fish tacos dorados, grilled lobster, and
  ceviche tostadas, paired with refreshing salsas and artisanal
  tortillas for a true taste of the region.

Grilled lobster

Artisana tortillas

International Dining

- **Fusion Cuisine:** Explore the innovative world of fusion cuisine in Cabo San Lucas, where chefs blend global culinary influences to create unique and exciting flavor combinations. From Asian-inspired tacos and sushi burritos to Mediterranean-infused seafood dishes and Latin-Asian fusion fare, fusion restaurants offer a culinary adventure that transcends borders.

Sushi burritos

- **European Fare:** Indulge in the elegance of European cuisine at upscale restaurants and bistros in Cabo San Lucas. From Italian trattorias and French brasseries to Spanish tapas bars and German beer gardens, European eateries serve up a delectable array of dishes crafted with precision and artistry.

Fine Dining

- **Gourmet Restaurants:** Treat yourself to an unforgettable dining experience at one of Cabo San Lucas's gourmet restaurants, where world-class chefs showcase their culinary expertise through innovative tasting menus and exquisite presentations. From oceanfront fine dining establishments to intimate chef's tables and exclusive wine pairings, gourmet restaurants offer a feast for the senses that delights both palate and spirit.

- Luxury Dining: Immerse yourself in the lap of luxury at Cabo's upscale dining venues, where opulent surroundings, impeccable service, and indulgent menus combine to create an unparalleled gastronomic experience. Whether you're celebrating a special occasion or simply seeking a taste of the high life, luxury dining establishments in Cabo San Lucas deliver an unforgettable culinary journey.

Casual Dining:
- Beachfront Eateries: Dine al fresco with your toes in the sand at one of Cabo San Lucas's laid-back beachfront eateries, where fresh seafood, ice-cold margaritas, and breathtaking views come together to create a quintessential Cabo experience. From rustic beach bars and seafood shacks to casual cafes and grill joints, beachfront eateries

offer a relaxed atmosphere and authentic flavors that capture the essence of Cabo's coastal lifestyle.

- Local Favorites: Discover hidden gems and neighborhood haunts beloved by locals, where you can enjoy hearty comfort food, authentic street tacos, and homemade specialties at affordable prices. From bustling taquerias and family-owned cafes to roadside stands and market stalls, local favorites offer a taste of genuine hospitality and community spirit.

Dining and cuisine in Cabo San Lucas is a culinary adventure waiting to be explored, with a rich tapestry of flavors, ingredients, and traditions that reflect the region's cultural diversity and natural abundance. Whether you're craving classic Mexican dishes, international fare, or gourmet delights, Cabo's dining scene offers a feast for the senses that will leave you craving more. So come hungry, pull up a chair, and prepare to embark on a culinary journey through the flavors of Cabo San Lucas.

SOME MAJOR MEALS FOUND IN CABO SAN LUCAS

Photos of meals to familiarize yourself with for the journey

Cochinita Pibil

Tamales

Mole

Quesadilla

Guacamole con Chapulines

Enchiladas

Chile en Nogada

Quesadilla

Aguachile

Tlayuda

Camarones a la Diabla

Flautas

Chilaquiles

Huevos Rancheros

Carnitas

Machaca

Torta Ahogada

Discada

Tacos

Burritos

Pozole

Menudo

Experience the Vibrant Nightlife and Entertainment Scene in Cabo San Lucas

As the sun sets over the Pacific Ocean, this Mexican paradise transforms into a playground for those seeking unforgettable entertainment and electrifying nightlife experiences.

The Marina District

The Marina District is the heart of Cabo's nightlife scene. Lined with an array of bars, clubs, and restaurants, it offers something for every taste and preference. From upscale lounges with panoramic views of the marina to lively cantinas pulsating with live music, the Marina District caters to both locals and tourists alike.

Cabo Wabo Cantina

No visit to Cabo San Lucas is complete without a stop at Cabo Wabo Cantina, the iconic nightlife destination founded by rock legend Sammy Hagar. This legendary cantina combines live music, delicious cocktails, and a lively atmosphere, making it a must-visit for music enthusiasts and partygoers.

The Golden Zone

view1

view 2

view 3

Located along the bustling Medano Beach, the Golden Zone is another hotspot for nightlife and entertainment. Here, you'll find an eclectic mix of beach clubs, bars, and restaurants offering everything from sunset cocktails to late-night dancing under the stars. With its lively ambiance and stunning ocean views, the Golden Zone promises an unforgettable evening out on the town.

El Squid Roe

For those seeking a truly immersive nightlife experience, El Squid Roe is the place to be. This multi-level nightclub boasts vibrant décor, energetic live performances, and a dance floor that never sleeps. Whether you're looking to dance the night away or simply soak in the lively atmosphere, El Squid Roe promises an exhilarating night of fun and excitement.

Live Music Venues

Cabo San Lucas is also home to a thriving live music scene, with an array of venues showcasing talented local musicians and international acts. From intimate jazz clubs to open-air amphitheaters, music enthusiasts can enjoy a diverse range of performances against the backdrop of Cabo's stunning scenery.

Sunset Cruises

For a more laid-back yet equally memorable evening, consider embarking on a sunset cruise along the coastline of Cabo San Lucas. Sip on cocktails, savor delicious cuisine, and dance to the rhythm of live music as you watch the sun dip below the horizon in a spectacular display of colors.

Whether you're in the mood for pulsating nightlife, live music, or a leisurely sunset cruise, Cabo has something for everyone, ensuring an unforgettable experience that will keep you coming back for more.

Major areas of sunset cruises in Cabo

El Arco (The Arch)

One of the most iconic landmarks of Cabo San Lucas, El Arco offers a breathtaking backdrop for sunset cruises. As the sun dips below the horizon, casting vibrant hues across the sky, witness the arch bathed in golden light. This natural rock formation at Land's End is a must-see spectacle and a perfect spot for capturing memorable sunset photographs.

Lover's Beach (Playa del Amor)

Sail along the coastline to Lover's Beach, a secluded paradise nestled between towering cliffs. As the day transitions into dusk, enjoy the tranquil ambiance of this idyllic retreat. The calm waters and picturesque surroundings make it an ideal location for a romantic sunset cruise. Watch as the sky transforms into a canvas of fiery colors, reflecting off the crystal-clear waters, creating a truly magical experience.

Medano Beach

Experience the vibrant energy of Medano Beach from the tranquility of a sunset cruise. As the boat glides along the coastline, soak in the panoramic views of the bustling beachfront, dotted with lively bars and restaurants. The sunset casts a warm glow over the lively scene, providing a unique perspective of this popular tourist destination. Raise a toast to the day's end as you marvel at the beauty of nature's nightly spectacle.

Santa Maria Bay

For a more serene sunset cruise experience, venture to Santa Maria Bay, a pristine cove known for its crystal-clear waters and vibrant marine life. Cruise along the rugged coastline, framed by towering cliffs and lush vegetation, as you witness the transition from day to night. The secluded setting offers a peaceful retreat from the hustle and bustle of Cabo San Lucas, allowing you to unwind and connect with nature amidst stunning surroundings.

Pelican Rock

Embark on a sunset cruise to Pelican Rock, a popular snorkeling spot located near Land's End. As the sun sets on the horizon, watch as the rugged rock formations are bathed in a warm, golden light. Keep an eye out for playful sea lions and colorful fish that inhabit the area, adding to the enchanting ambiance of the sunset cruise. With its pristine waters and dramatic scenery, Pelican Rock offers a memorable setting to enjoy nature's nightly spectacle.

See more photos:

Chileno Bay

Set sail to Chileno Bay and experience a sunset cruise surrounded by natural beauty and tranquility. The pristine waters of this marine sanctuary provide the perfect setting for watching the sun sink below the horizon. As the sky transforms into a palette of vibrant colors, take in the serenity of the bay and appreciate the untouched beauty of the surrounding landscape. Whether you're seeking romance or relaxation, Chileno Bay offers an unforgettable sunset cruise experience in Cabo San Lucas.

Trips and Excursions

Boat tours in Cabo San Lucas

1. Land's End Cruise

Embark on a thrilling adventure along the dramatic coastline of Land's End on a boat tour in Cabo San Lucas. Marvel at iconic landmarks such as El Arco, Lover's Beach, and the majestic sea lion colony as you cruise past towering rock formations and pristine beaches. Keep your camera ready to capture unforgettable moments against the backdrop of the sparkling Sea of Cortez and the Pacific Ocean. Whether you choose a luxury yacht or a traditional panga boat, a Land's End cruise promises a memorable experience for all.

2. Snorkeling Excursions

Discover the vibrant underwater world of Cabo San Lucas on a snorkeling boat tour. Cruise to pristine snorkeling spots such as Santa Maria Bay, Chileno Bay, or Pelican Rock, where crystal-clear waters teem with colorful marine life. Dive into the sea and explore coral reefs, tropical fish, and even encounter friendly sea lions in their natural habitat. With professional guides and top-notch snorkeling gear provided, these excursions are suitable for snorkelers of all skill levels, making it a perfect activity for families and adventure seekers alike.

3. Sunset Sailing

Indulge in romance and relaxation with a sunset sailing tour in Cabo San Lucas. Set sail aboard a luxurious catamaran or sailboat and watch as the sky transforms into a canvas of vibrant colors during the golden hour. Toast to the day's end with a glass of champagne or a tropical cocktail as you soak in panoramic views of the coastline and landmarks like El Arco and Land's End. With the gentle sea breeze and the sound of waves as your backdrop, a sunset sailing tour offers the perfect blend of tranquility and luxury.

4. Whale Watching Expeditions

Embark on an unforgettable whale watching adventure in the waters surrounding Cabo San Lucas. Join expert guides on a boat tour to witness the annual migration of majestic humpback whales, gray whales, and even the occasional blue whale. Marvel at these gentle giants breaching, tail-slapping, and spouting just a few feet away from your boat. With informative commentary provided by knowledgeable naturalists, you'll gain insights into the behavior and biology of these magnificent marine mammals. Don't miss the opportunity to witness one of nature's most awe-inspiring spectacles on a whale watching expedition in Cabo.

5. Private Charters

For a personalized and exclusive experience, consider booking a private charter boat tour in Cabo San Lucas. Whether you're celebrating a special occasion or simply seeking privacy and flexibility, a private charter allows you to tailor your itinerary and amenities to your preferences. Choose from a variety of vessels, including luxury yachts, sportfishing boats, or traditional Mexican pangas, and embark on a customized adventure tailored to your interests. Whether you're fishing, snorkeling, or simply cruising along the coastline, a private charter ensures a truly memorable and intimate experience on the waters of Cabo San Lucas.

Wildlife encounters in Cabo San Lucas excursions

1. Whale Watching Tours

Embark on a thrilling whale watching excursion in Cabo San Lucas to witness the majestic giants of the sea. From December to April, the waters off the coast of Cabo become a haven for migrating humpback whales, gray whales, and even the occasional blue whale. Join experienced guides on boat tours as they navigate the waters in search of these awe-inspiring creatures. Watch in awe as whales breach, slap their tails, and spout water into the air, providing a once-in-a-lifetime wildlife encounter that will leave you spellbound.

2. Sea Turtle Release Programs

Participate in a conservation effort by joining a sea turtle release program in Cabo San Lucas. During certain times of the year, conservation organizations allow visitors to assist in releasing newly hatched sea turtles into the ocean. Learn about the lifecycle of these endangered creatures and the conservation efforts aimed at protecting them. As you release baby turtles into the sea, you'll not only contribute to their survival but also witness a heartwarming moment of nature in action.

3. Snorkeling with Sea Lions

Immerse yourself in the playful world of sea lions with a snorkeling excursion in Cabo San Lucas. Cruise to remote sea lion colonies where these charismatic marine mammals frolic in their natural habitat. Don your snorkeling gear and plunge into the crystal-clear waters to swim alongside these curious creatures. Watch as they glide effortlessly through the water, twirl playfully, and even come in for a closer look at their human visitors. With the guidance of experienced guides, you'll have the opportunity to observe sea lions up close while respecting their natural environment.

4. Birdwatching Tours

Discover the diverse birdlife of Cabo San Lucas on a bird watching excursion that takes you to hidden gems off the beaten path. From colorful tropical birds to majestic raptors, the region is home to a wide variety of avian species. Join expert guides as they lead you to prime bird watching locations, including estuaries, wetlands, and desert oases. Keep your binoculars ready to spot species such as herons, egrets, pelicans, and even the endemic Cape pygmy owl. Whether you're a seasoned birder or a novice enthusiast, a birdwatching tour offers a rewarding opportunity to connect with nature and observe the winged wonders of Cabo.

5. Desert Safaris

Embark on a desert safari adventure to encounter the diverse wildlife that inhabits the arid landscapes surrounding Cabo San Lucas. Journey into the rugged terrain of the Baja California desert aboard off-road vehicles, traversing sandy dunes and rocky trails in search of elusive creatures. Keep your eyes peeled for desert wildlife such as roadrunners, desert iguanas, bighorn sheep, and even the iconic desert fox. With the backdrop of stunning desert vistas and the guidance of knowledgeable naturalist guides, a desert safari promises an unforgettable wildlife encounter in Cabo San Lucas.

Excursion to the historical site of Cabo San Lucas

Exploring the Historic Heart of Cabo San Lucas

Embark on a journey through time with a guided excursion to explore the rich history and cultural heritage of Cabo San Lucas. Delve into the fascinating past of this coastal gem as you visit its most iconic historical sites, revealing tales of conquest, colonization, and resilience.

1. Land's End and El Arco

Begin your excursion with a scenic boat ride to Land's End, where you'll encounter the iconic rock formation known as El Arco. As you cruise along the coastline, marvel at the rugged beauty of this natural wonder, which has served as a navigational landmark for sailors and explorers for centuries. Learn about the significance of El Arco in the maritime history of Cabo San Lucas and its role in shaping the cultural identity of the region.

2. San Lucas Church (Iglesia de San Lucas)

Next, journey into the heart of downtown Cabo San Lucas to visit the historic San Lucas Church, also known as Iglesia de San Lucas. Dating back to the 18th century, this charming colonial-era church stands as a symbol of faith and community in the region. Step inside to admire its rustic architecture, ornate altars, and religious artwork, and learn about the role of Catholicism in shaping the cultural landscape of Cabo San Lucas.

3. Old Town Cabo San Lucas

Stroll through the quaint streets of Old Town Cabo San Lucas, where colonial-era buildings and cobblestone plazas evoke a sense of bygone charm. Explore historic landmarks such as Plaza

Amelia Wilkes and Plaza Mijares, where locals gather to socialize and celebrate cultural events. Along the way, discover hidden gems like Casa de la Cultura, a cultural center housed in a historic building that offers exhibitions, workshops, and performances showcasing the artistic heritage of Cabo San Lucas.

4. Museo de las Californias

Step back in time at the Museo de las Californias, a museum dedicated to preserving the history and heritage of Baja California Sur. Browse through exhibits that chronicle the region's indigenous cultures, colonial period, and modern development, featuring artifacts, photographs, and interactive displays. Gain insights into the diverse influences that have shaped the identity of Cabo San Lucas, from ancient civilizations to Spanish colonization to contemporary tourism.

5. Marina Cabo San Lucas

Conclude your historical excursion with a visit to Marina Cabo San Lucas, a bustling waterfront area that blends old-world charm with modern amenities. Admire the luxury yachts and fishing boats that line the marina while soaking in panoramic views of the Sea of Cortez. Reflect on the centuries of maritime history that have shaped Cabo San Lucas as you enjoy a leisurely stroll along the waterfront promenade, dotted with shops, restaurants, and cafes.

6. San José del Cabo Mission (Mission San José del Cabo Añuití)

The San José del Cabo Mission, also known as Mission San José del Cabo Anuití, stands as a testament to the rich history and cultural heritage of the region. Located in the charming town of San José del Cabo, this historic site dates back to the 18th century when it was founded by Jesuit missionaries.

Constructed in 1730, the mission was established with the primary purpose of converting the indigenous inhabitants of the area to Christianity. The mission served as a hub for religious activities, education, and agriculture, playing a vital role in the Spanish colonization of Baja California.

The architecture of the San José del Cabo Mission is a blend of Spanish colonial and indigenous influences, featuring adobe walls, a traditional bell tower, and a simple yet elegant interior adorned with religious artwork and symbols. The mission's rustic charm and serene atmosphere offer visitors a glimpse into the region's colonial past and the enduring legacy of Catholicism in Baja California.

Today, the San José del Cabo Mission remains an active parish church and a cherished historical landmark. Visitors can explore the mission grounds, attend Mass, and admire the architectural details and religious artifacts that reflect centuries of history and tradition.

Surrounded by picturesque streets, colorful buildings, and vibrant plazas, the San José del Cabo Mission serves as a focal point of cultural and spiritual significance in the heart of downtown San José del Cabo. Whether you're a history enthusiast, a religious pilgrim, or simply a curious traveler, a visit to this iconic historical site offers a glimpse into the enduring legacy of faith and heritage in Cabo San Lucas.

Embark on this immersive excursion to uncover the hidden treasures and timeless tales of Cabo San Lucas' historical heritage. Whether you're a history buff, a cultural enthusiast, or simply a curious traveler, this journey through the past promises to deepen your appreciation for the rich tapestry of experiences that define this captivating destination.
See more photos:

170

Tips for a Memorable Trip

1. Plan Ahead
Research and plan your itinerary in advance to make the most of your time in San Lucas. Identify must-see attractions, activities, and dining experiences, and consider making reservations for popular tours and restaurants to avoid disappointment.

2. Embrace the Local Cuisine
Indulge in the vibrant flavors of Baja California by sampling local cuisine. From fresh seafood tacos to savory ceviche and traditional Mexican dishes, San Lucas offers a diverse culinary scene that caters to all tastes. Don't miss the opportunity to dine at authentic eateries and street food stalls to savor the true essence of the region's gastronomy.

3. Stay Hydrated and Sun-Protected
San Lucas enjoys a sunny and warm climate year-round, so it's essential to stay hydrated and sun-protected during your trip. Pack plenty of water, wear sunscreen, a hat, and sunglasses, and seek shade during the hottest hours of the day to prevent sunburn and dehydration.

4. Explore Beyond the Tourist Hotspots

While San Lucas boasts famous landmarks and attractions, take the time to explore beyond the tourist hotspots. Wander through charming neighborhoods, discover hidden beaches, and interact with locals to gain a deeper appreciation for the culture and lifestyle of the region.

5. Engage in Outdoor Adventures

Take advantage of San Lucas's stunning natural beauty by engaging in outdoor adventures. Whether it's snorkeling in crystal-clear waters, hiking through desert landscapes, or zip-lining over lush canopies, there's no shortage of thrilling activities to enjoy in San Lucas. Embrace your sense of adventure and create unforgettable memories in the great outdoors.

6. Respect Local Customs and Etiquette

Show respect for local customs and etiquette during your trip to San Lucas. Learn a few basic phrases in Spanish, greet locals with a friendly "hola," and be mindful of cultural sensitivities. Additionally, dress modestly when visiting religious sites and always ask for permission before taking photos of people.

7. Stay Safe and Aware

Prioritize your safety and well-being while exploring San Lucas. Be vigilant of your surroundings, especially in crowded areas and tourist hotspots. Keep your belongings secure, avoid walking alone at night in unfamiliar areas, and heed any safety warnings or advisories issued by local authorities.

8. Capture Memories

Document your adventures in San Lucas by capturing photos and videos of your experiences. Whether you're snapping shots of breathtaking landscapes, sampling delicious cuisine, or making new friends along the way, photos serve as cherished mementos that allow you to relive your trip for years to come.

By following these tips, you'll be well-equipped to create lasting memories and have a truly memorable trip in San Lucas. Enjoy every moment of your adventure and embrace the beauty and culture of this enchanting destination!

CONCLUSION

As we reach the conclusion of our journey through the vibrant landscapes and rich cultural tapestry of Cabo San Lucas, it's evident that this enchanting destination is more than just a tropical getaway—it's a treasure trove of experiences waiting to be explored.

Throughout this travel guide, we've delved into the sun-kissed beaches, azure waters, and rugged desert terrain that define the natural beauty of Cabo San Lucas. From the iconic landmarks of Land's End and El Arco to the hidden gems of Santa Maria Bay and Chileno Bay, each location tells a story of adventure, relaxation, and natural wonder.

But beyond its stunning landscapes, Cabo San Lucas is a melting pot of culture, history, and culinary delights. We've sampled the flavors of Baja California, from mouthwatering seafood tacos to zesty margaritas, and immersed ourselves in the colorful streets and lively plazas that pulse with the rhythm of Mexican life.

As we bid farewell to this captivating destination, let us carry with us the memories of sunsets painted in hues of gold and crimson, the laughter of new friends made on sandy shores, and the sense of wonder that comes from exploring a place steeped in history and tradition.

Whether you're a seasoned traveler seeking adventure or a weary soul in need of rejuvenation, Cabo San Lucas beckons with open arms, ready to unveil its treasures and secrets to those who dare to seek them. So, as you embark on your own journey to this jewel of Baja, may you find inspiration, relaxation, and countless moments of magic awaiting you in the sun-drenched paradise of Cabo San Lucas. ¡Hasta luego y buen viaje!

Made in United States
Orlando, FL
16 June 2024

47949700R00098